MGOV
NO LOANS

Reclaiming Multilateralism

For People, Rights and Sustainable Development

by Barbara Adams and Gretchen Luchsinger

BIBLIOTHÈQUES
DÉPÔT
DEPOSIT
UNIVERSITY
LIBRARIES

UNITED NATIONS
Geneva and New York, 2012

NGLS
UN Non-Governmental Liaison Service

Generalitat de Catalunya

The responsibility for views and ideas expressed in this publication rests solely with the authors, and publication does not constitute an endorsement by the United Nations Non-Governmental Liaison Service or any other part of the UN system of the opinions expressed.

NGLS publications are published for non-governmental and civil society organizations and others interested in the institutions, policies, and activities of the UN's agenda, including economic and social development, human rights, environment, peace and security. This publication, and all other NGLS publications, can be found on the NGLS website (www.un-ngls.org). Text from this publication may be reproduced unaltered without authorization on condition that the source is indicated. For rights of reproduction or translation, application should be made to NGLS, Palais des Nations, 1211 Geneva 10, Switzerland.

Photo credits: Fotolia

UNCTAD/NGLS/2012/1

Sales No. E.12.II.D.8
ISBN: 978-92-1-112849-9
e-ISBN: 978-92-1-055427-5

©2012 United Nations. All rights reserved.
Published in April 2012 by
UN Non-Governmental Liaison Service (NGLS)
Palais des Nations, CH-1211 Geneva 10, Switzerland
Room DC1-1106, United Nations, New York NY 10017, United States

NO LOANS
UN2
TD/UNCTAD/NGLS/2012/1

"Several global crises (in finances, climate and food) are merging into an unprecedented storm which the international institutions are unprepared to cope with. Barbara Adams and Gretchen Luchsinger argue with precise wording and passionate commitment that multilateralism as we know it needs to be re-founded –or, in their own words, *reclaimed*. People, rights and sustainable development are being paid lip service by all. This book shows how to make the multilateral system work to actually promote them. The proposal is surprisingly simple if only we dare to introduce *coherence* between the promises and the actions."

Roberto Bissio, Coordinator of Social Watch

Acknowledgements

NGLS gratefully acknowledges the generous support of the Government of Catalonia in making this publication possible. The authors would like to thank Karen Judd, Alison Drayton, Gigi Francisco, Roberto Bissio and Hamish Jenkins for their substantive inputs. The authors would also like to acknowledge the work of the Civil Society Reflection Group on Global Development Perspectives and express appreciation for their discussions on many of the core ideas developed in the publication. Many thanks also go to all NGLS staff for their initiation and support for this project: Tomás Gonzalez, Jolanda Groen, Beth Peoc'h and David Vergari.

Table of Contents

Acronyms

ASEAN	Association of Southeast Asian Nations
AU	African Union
BRICS	Brazil, Russia, India, China & South Africa
BWIs	Bretton Woods Institutions
CFS	Committee on World Food Security
CSM	Civil Society Mechanism
DAC	Development Assistance Committee
G-20	Group of 20
EU	European Union
FAO	Food and Agriculture Organization of the United Nations
GATT	General Agreement on Tariffs and Trade
GDP	Gross Domestic Product
IBRD	International Bank for Reconstruction and Development
IFIs	International Financial Institutions
ILO	International Labour Organization
IMF	International Monetary Fund
ITU	International Telegraph Union
MDGs	Millennium Development Goals
NGLS	United Nations Non-Governmental Liaison Service
NGO	Non-Governmental Organization
ODA	Official Development Assistance
OECD	Organisation for Economic Co-operation and Development
UN	United Nations
UNASUR	Union of South American Nations
UNCED	United Nations Conference on Environment and Development
UPR	Universal Periodic Review
UPU	Universal Postal Union
WTO	World Trade Organization

Preface

The year 2011 was characterized by new social movements around the world expressing discontent with political and economic systems and calling for justice and fairness in widely varying contexts. The recent finding that three-quarters of the world's poor people are actually living in middle-income countries is a testament to the failure of the economic-growth-only model adopted and promoted by dominant parts of the multilateral system and individual nations. In other words, economies have grown, but the prospects for most people have not. The ongoing global economic crisis is resulting in more poverty, more exclusion, more instability and more inequality in developing and developed countries alike, and has enlarged the crisis to a social and political one. A host of other challenges are already being faced by the global community – climate change and its consequences, food insecurity and fuel shortages, patterns of unsustainable development and consumption – which further aggravate the situation.

These global challenges need to be addressed urgently. *Reclaiming Multilateralism*, authored by Barbara Adams and Gretchen Luchsinger, argues that the structural transformations required to equitably share the benefits of wealth creation and to balance progress across all three pillars of sustainable development (economic, social and environmental) will not be achieved without a multilateral system equipped for that end. It notes that multilateral institutions have not matched the pace of global change and that the balance needed between "realism" and "idealism" in the interest of achieving common human rights and sustainable development goals has been increasingly off. It cautions that multilateralism has been seen by some powerful States primarily as a means for securing short-term political and economic interests in a competitive world, which significantly reduces the scope of debate and the prospects for globally beneficial action. Instead it feeds tensions around multilateralism related to individual countries' sovereignty and policy space.

While the publication highlights that multilateralism, in its simplest form, involves more than two sovereign countries working together on a given issue, many more actors have entered the global development debate in the past decades, demanding a more inclusive space to share relevant insights and to influence multilateral decision-making processes. Although many multilateral organizations have opened their doors to other actors, including civil society, the private sector and academia, many voices remain under-represented, including those of sub-national governments and social movements, even though they often represent people most affected by multilateral decisions or omissions. A multilateral system that is far more effective and inclusive than the one in place today is needed.

Reclaiming Multilateralism sets off on an exploration of what multilateralism should and could look like when sufficient political will is in place to make the necessary changes. It raises as many questions as answers, aiming to generate further thinking. The publication includes three chapters. While Chapter 1 looks at multilateralism from its beginning to the present and asks a series of conceptual questions on reform, and Chapter 3 provides recommendations for specific actions, Chapter 2 challenges the reader to imagine the ideal. What would it mean if the multilateral system was realigned around the principles of human rights and the three pillars of sustainable development? What would a broader vision of multilateral decision-making entail in terms of rebalancing realism and idealism that is in line with sustainable development and the global collective good?

NGLS seeks to contribute to the on-going dialogue of the international development community through the dissemination of challenging analyses and reflections from independent observers and authors on key current issues on the international development agenda. This NGLS publication therefore aims to engage all stakeholders – whether government, multilateral, regional, and sub-national institutions, civil society and social movements – in an open debate on a "new multilateralism" or rather what kinds of development and governance models the multilateral system should be endorsing that would re-balance and regulate the political, economic and social shifts brought by globalization and bring the promises of justice, equity and sustainable development to fruition.

Beth Peoc'h
Officer-in-Charge
United Nations Non-Governmental Liaison Service

ntroduction

In 2012, UN Member States are conducting a 20-year review of the landmark United Nations Conference on Environment and Development (UNCED) and its outcome agreements, the Rio Declaration and Agenda 21. When these agreements were struck in Rio de Janeiro in 1992, they represented a breakthrough in multilateral consensus. Raising the bar for political commitment, they established the concept of sustainable development as comprising three pillars – social, economic and environmental – that must be dealt with together. All signatories agreed they had common but differentiated responsibilities to implement steps to achieve sustainable development, meaning they must all work towards that end, but those with greater resources and capacities are obligated to do more.

> LITTLE HAS BEEN DONE TO CHANGE PATTERNS OF PRODUCTION AND CONSUMPTION THAT POLLUTE, ERODE BIODIVERSITY AND LEAD INEXORABLY TO CLIMATE CHANGE.

Over the last 20 years, however, the ideals and principles of Rio have been overshadowed as implementation has mostly not occurred. Similarly, a host of commitments to international human and women's rights have not been fulfilled. Some economies have grown at double-digit rates, yet with widening disparities. Globalization has yielded millions of poor quality jobs. Little has been done to change patterns of production and consumption that pollute, erode biodiversity and lead inexorably to climate change.

The Rio Conference, like other multilateral forums, underscored that the multilateral system should be the focal point for systematically acting on issues of global concern. *Reclaiming Multilateralism* sets out to explore why that system today has reached a point where it is more needed than ever before, but in light of worsening trends in sustainable development and human rights, very real questions should be raised about its relevance. In a concise format intended for civil society audiences, as well as government and UN representatives, the publication considers how the multilateral system could realign itself around commitments to human rights and sustainable development, and recommends some concrete steps in that direction.

Critiques of the multilateral system come from many directions. While there is a tendency to look within multilateral institutions for the solutions to an array of problems, *Reclaiming Multilateralism* maintains that if the goal of the multilateral system is to achieve human rights and all three pillars of sustainable development, the starting point for any critique needs to be the context in which the multilateral system operates. The following pages explore how an unsustainable economic model has allowed a few powerful countries and political elites to dominate multilateral debates. These interests have gained most from patterns of globalization associated with deeply inequitable benefits and costs. They have also become firmly entrenched, in the era of global interdependency, as "too big to fail." This makes them virtually untouchable, even by the collective will of the multilateral system, and even on issues where global well-being is at stake.

In looking primarily at their own interests, powerful countries are well within the tradition of political realism. But they have lost the connection to another tradition – of adhering to ideals based on higher human aspirations. As long as there are nation States, all countries will be able to justify the pursuit of sovereign national interest. This publication argues, however, that competing needs of global significance must be fairly and equitably moderated through a multilateral system that is far more effective than the one in place today.

Such a system would re-balance realism with a collective idealism, in which universally endorsed principles of human rights and sustainable development would take the lead. It would be guided by the recognition that there are diverse ways of realizing the same objectives, and that individual interests will always be there, but need to be aligned with collective imperatives.

Reclaiming Multilateralism embarks on an exploration of multilateralism with as many questions as answers, aiming to provoke further thought. The book is divided into three chapters. The first looks at the past and present of multilateralism. It analyses some of the underlying reasons why multilateral governance has not lived up to human rights and sustainable development objectives, notably in relation to contemporaneous issues of power and participation, flawed development models and major fault-lines plaguing the multilateral system today.

A series of questions at the end of the chapter ask readers to consider four concepts often used in multilateral reform discussions, but requiring much deeper analysis than is the norm – namely, effectiveness, representation, accountability and neutrality.

Chapter 2 considers what it might mean if the multilateral system was realigned around the principles of human rights and all three pillars of sustainable development. The chapter is intended to imagine the ideal.

Chapter 3 grounds the discussion with recommendations for specific actions that aim high but could be taken now – towards a longer-term vision of change. Most of the actions will be the responsibility of government leaders and policy makers. But all multilateral stakeholders, including civil society, can use the recommendations to campaign for a new multilateralism, where the promises of justice, equity and sustainable development can finally be fulfilled.

1 Moving Forward,
Stopping (Way) Short

Multilateralism, in its simplest definition, involves more than two sovereign countries working together on a given issue. While multilateralism in various configurations has been around since the formation of nation States, it was not until the mid-1800s that governments created the first international institutions – the International Telegraph Union (ITU) and the Universal Postal Union (UPU).

It took another 80 years, and two world wars, before the United Nations became an umbrella institution for multilateral debate and action. In 1944, the United Nations Monetary and Financial Conference, commonly known as the Bretton Woods Conference, took place. It set up the International Bank for Reconstruction and Development (IBRD), the first institution of what is now known as the World Bank Group; the General Agreement on Tariffs and Trade (GATT), superseded in 1995 by the World Trade Organization (WTO); and the International Monetary Fund (IMF).

> MULTILATERALISM, IN ITS SIMPLEST DEFINITION, INVOLVES MORE THAN TWO SOVEREIGN COUNTRIES WORKING TOGETHER ON A GIVEN ISSUE.

Foundations of the United Nations

A compelling priority for the fledgling UN, in the wake of World War II, was to help maintain peace. The theory was that if nations could come together and talk it would reduce the probability of war. This was not the only foundational objective set out in the UN Charter, however. There are four:

- To save succeeding generations from the scourge of war;

- To reaffirm faith in fundamental human rights;

- To establish conditions for upholding international law; and

- To promote social progress and better standards of life in larger freedom.

The Charter specifically mandates the United Nations to promote: higher standards of living, full employment, and conditions of economic and social progress and development; solutions of international economic, social, health and related problems; international cultural and educational cooperation; and universal respect for, and observance of, human rights and fundamental freedoms for all without distinction as to race, sex, language or religion.[1] The Charter was followed by the Universal Declaration of Human Rights, and a series of conventions with specific commitments to economic, social, civil, political and cultural rights.

The landmark 1992 Earth Summit

In 1992, the United Nations Conference on Environment and Development (UNCED), or "Earth Summit," encapsulated many multilateral aspirations in the concept of sustainable development (see Box 1), which rests on three pillars: economic development, social development and the protection of the environment as a resource necessary for human survival. Agenda 21, UNCED's programme of action, stipulated that all three are interconnected and must be addressed together. The accompanying Rio Declaration defined the principle of common but differentiated responsibility, where States with greater resources and capacities have greater responsibilities.

An inherent tension: realism versus collective idealism

Today's multilateral institutions are part of a system of global governance, which is distinct from global government. Global governance entails sovereign States agreeing on international norms and rules, the means for implementation, and accountability mechanisms to uphold them. National governments use multilateral forums to identify and agree on these norms, as well as on how to implement them. Some standards can be enforced through the "hard" power of institutions and binding treaties; others through the "soft" power of networks, consensus and peer pressure.

Historically, multilateralism has been influenced by two competing tendencies: **realism** (or realpolitik), where States act to advance their own interests, and a **collective idealism**, where States orient their actions around larger principles of human rights and the common good. A mixture of these two tendencies has typically been the norm, but the balance is often off, including where the reference points are human rights and sustainable development. Many multilateral actions have been under-ambitious given the principles they aim to uphold. Others, overly optimistic in expectations for implementation, have fallen short of their potential.

Box 1

WHAT IS SUSTAINABLE DEVELOPMENT?

The 1992 UN Conference on Environment and Development – otherwise known as UNCED, the Rio Conference or the Earth Summit – had several outcomes. Besides Agenda 21, signed by 178 UN Member States, and the Rio Declaration, which outlined guiding principles, the Conference adopted a Statement of Principles for the Sustainable Management of Forests, and launched three conventions on climate change, biodiversity and desertification. All three conventions have since come into force.

The Rio Declaration endorsed a number of principles that have become central to international environmental law, but that could be more broadly applied to sustainable development and human rights. They include:

Common but differentiated responsibility: In view of the different contributions to global environmental degradation, States have common but differentiated responsibilities. The developed countries acknowledge the responsibility that they bear in the international pursuit of sustainable development in view of the pressures their societies place on the global environment and of the technologies and financial resources they command.

Public participation: Environmental issues are best handled with the participation of all concerned citizens, at the relevant level. At the national level, each individual shall have appropriate access to information...that is held by public authorities...and the opportunity to participate in public decision-making processes. States shall facilitate and encourage public awareness and participation by making information widely available.

Precautionary principle: In order to protect the environment, the precautionary approach shall be widely applied by States according to their capabilities. Where there are threats of serious or irreversible damage, lack of full scientific certainty shall not be used as a reason for postponing cost-effective measures to prevent environmental degradation.

Ending unsustainable consumption and production: To achieve sustainable development and a higher quality of life for all people, States should reduce and eliminate unsustainable patterns of production and consumption and promote appropriate demographic policies.

Polluter pays: The polluter should, in principle, bear the cost of pollution, with due regard to the public interest and without distorting international trade and investment.

Source: Rio Declaration, Principles 7, 8, 10, 15, 16

Multilateralism today: power

Since the UN Charter was signed, the UN has channeled multilateral commitment and resources into a variety of achievements possible only through broad-based action. They include but are not limited to:

- Resolving and preventing conflicts, and slowing nuclear proliferation;

- Shepherding the process of decolonization;

- Strengthening international law;

- Setting new, higher standards for sustainable development, human rights and environmental protection, many of which have been translated into national laws and policies by UN Member States;

- Challenging established notions of economic development and offering alternatives centred on equity and people's well-being; and

- Convening diverse groups of stakeholders who might otherwise not engage each other.

Despite these achievements, multilateral institutions and the aspirations for them have not matched the pace of global change or new rationales for multilateral engagement emerging from global challenges. Most of the main institutions today remain those that came into being around World War II. Although achieving human rights and sustainable development requires integrated actions, they operate in separate arenas. The UN retains its development, peace and security, and human rights mandate. The World Bank and IMF deal primarily with economic development issues, and international monetary and financial cooperation, respectively. The WTO regulates trade, brokers trade agreements and manages a dispute resolution mechanism.

The UN remains the most inclusive, broad-based multilateral institution. Each of its 193 Member States has a vote in the General Assembly, although the Security Council still has the same permanent five members – China, France, Russia, the United Kingdom and the United States – that reflect the post-World War II balance of global power. At the IMF and the World Bank, participation and governance remain linked to political and economic clout, with the United States as the dominant power, despite recent global economic shifts that have given a somewhat greater say to Brazil, China and India as emerging economies.

Challenges to inclusive multilateralism

In general, the last several years have witnessed a retreat from inclusive multilateralism. A number of current critiques centre on the process of political decision-making, with inclusive bodies such as the UN General Assembly deemed inefficient and subject to the disproportionate influence of smaller States due to the one-country, one-vote system.

In response to these perceived deficiencies, more exclusive groupings are being applied to discussions that impact the vast majority of people, such as those about the global economy and its implications for development. The most recent example is the **G-20,**[2] which grew in prominence after convening member Heads of State and Government to coordinate a response to the 2008 global financial crisis. By 2010, it was describing itself as "the premier forum for our international economic cooperation."[3] Another emerging group is the **BRICS** – Brazil, Russia, India, China and South Africa. It has raised some important economic issues that have not been adequately addressed in other multilateral forums. Like the G-20, however, to which all of these countries belong, it still speaks mainly for large, powerful States.

For its part, the G-20 does represent the most economically powerful countries, which also contain two-thirds of the world's population. But the Group's preoccupation so far has been with restarting economic growth – without drawing the lessons from the failed economic model that caused the 2008 global financial crisis – and which continue to encourage patterns of production and consumption that undermine sustainable development. By 2010, the Group added its Multi-Year Action Plan on Development to the now crowded landscape of development frameworks, highlighting infrastructure, market access and private investment, with scant attention to inequalities, human rights and sustainability.[4] By some accounts, the G-20 mainly reflects a new "oligarchy of power"[5] shared by the developed States and some rapidly emerging developing economies – and in particular by elite political and economic interests in both of them.

 Lack of implementation of its own decisions, including by its own members, have more recently cast doubts as to any perceived "comparative advantage" of the G-20 in terms of "effectiveness" vis-à-vis the "legitimacy" of bodies with universal membership like the United Nations.

In the best case scenario, multilateralism should aim to moderate power and interests, and balance idealism and realism in the interest of achieving common sustainable development goals. It should be premised on fairness in decision-making, where everyone agrees to consistently abide by common rules and values. Instead, pragmatism has trumped principles in current practice. Powerful States today see the purpose of multilateralism as primarily for securing short-term national interests in a competitive world. Even in forums designed to be more broadly inclusive, a few powerful interests can often dominate – and reduce the scope of debate and the prospects for globally beneficial action.

For less powerful States, the multilateral arena now seems full of contradictions and double standards, and is less and less trusted. More are emphasizing national and regional initiatives. A number of middle-sized developing countries have reduced engagement in multilateral processes and have adopted a defensive posture in political negotiations, working for a weak or non-committal result.

Regional approaches to inclusive multilateralism

Alternative approaches to global multilateralism have arisen on the premise of involving only those players – States and others – with the greatest stakes in a given issue, and thus theoretically the most powerful incentives to act in responding to it. Functional multilateralism, for instance, centres on a given task, such as regional cooperation on economic, social and environmental issues. Examples of regional multilateralism include the European Union (EU), the African Union (AU), the Association of Southeast Asian Nations (ASEAN) and more recently, the Union of South American Nations (UNASUR). These forms of regional multilateralism may play a complementary role on issues without global ramifications – but not only: they may also act as a countervailing force to global governance arrangements when these are perceived to be suffering from power imbalances and democratic deficits.

Regional multilateralism has the potential to be more inclusive – by giving a greater voice to smaller countries, especially on trade and financial issues – but experience shows that this is by no means automatic. Regional arrangements can suffer the same power imbalances and democratic deficits, especially when corporate interests are allowed, *de jure* or *de facto*, to trump human rights prerogatives.

Multilateralism today: participation

If power has become increasingly consolidated in the multilateral system, it is also true that an unprecedented number of stakeholders are now active in it. After major UN agreements, notably Agenda 21, began specifying the responsibilities of a variety of stakeholders in achieving sustainable development,[6] several multilateral institutions and some governments proactively encouraged the engagement of civil society groups, sub-national authorities, the private sector and academic experts (see Box 2, page 16). Over the past decade or so, ever-evolving technology has further spurred communication and networking (see Box 3, page 18).

A forum to claim justice and legitimacy

Today's multilateral stakeholders come with an array of incentives. Some want to make multilateralism work because they see it as the only way to negotiate complex global challenges with chances of achieving the fairest outcomes. Others focus on multilateral advocacy to gain traction on specific issues, especially where progress might be much slower on the national level. Groups facing longstanding social discrimination, including, among others, women, indigenous peoples and people with disabilities,[7] have all successfully advocated for new international commitments to outlaw discrimination and uphold their rights.

Tensions around multilateralism, "sovereignty" and "policy space"

Depending on which multilateral normative framework is referred to, stakeholders with divergent interests can also clash over the same international agreement. Political isolationists can disparage international human rights agreements as a threat to national sovereignty. Farmers' movements can campaign for the realization of the same human rights treaties while denouncing aspects of a number of international trade agreements as a threat to "food sovereignty." Those who benefit from the same trade agreements and enforcement of corporate and intellectual property rights are often the same transnational business and financial interests that oppose stronger corporate accountability standards and regulations.

These conflicting interests are a reflection of the growing debate around multilateralism and "policy space." Are there multilateral disciplines that impede the ability of governments to fulfill their human rights and sustainable development commitments? Is the absence of multilateral rules in certain areas, such as the regulation of finance and capital flows, shrinking the policy space to achieve the same commitments?

Benefits of diverse multistakeholder participation

Diverse participation in multilateralism has its inherent benefits. It brings together a wealth of different perspectives and capacities needed to achieve human rights and sustainable development, and to counteract forces that stand in the way. Many stakeholders offer valuable resources and expertise, as well unique capacities for broad political mobilization and accountability in the implementation of agreed decisions.

Risks of fragmentation and "lip service" participation

At the same time, this diversity has the potential for reinforcing fragmentation in setting priorities and goals, or funding and implementing strategies to achieve them. Accountability for achieving human rights and sustainable development is often not clear, never comprehensive and lacks appropriate mechanisms for enforcement. Some multistakeholder participation exercises serve mainly as a political cover for powerful interests intent on driving forward their own agendas, allowing little scope for the meaningful inclusion of alternative views and information in actual decisions or their implementation. Others simply suffer from the benign neglect of "lip service" participation resulting from bureaucratic routines devoid of genuine interests in impacting on the political process.

A Growing Sub-national Role

Box 2

The notion that the multilateral arena needs to extend beyond national governments gained ground at UNCED, where Agenda 21 emphasized that local governments and authorities make important contributions to sustainable development, including through the provision of public services and local environmental management. Since then, sub-national bodies such as municipal governments have been involved in UNCED follow up, including by creating local Agenda 21 action plans.

At the local level, where political configurations and the design of services can correspond more immediately to local demand, there can be room for innovation and greater ownership. Environmental stewardship is frequently a local pursuit because many threats to the environment are most readily felt close to home. In a number of countries, the process of decentralizing public services from central to local governments has given municipalities a far greater role in guiding local development.

Like some other multilateral stakeholders, sub-national authorities have perspectives that are not always reflected in national negotiations. This has been an incentive for them to engage with multilateral forums making decisions that affect them. They may have more reasons to do so if urbanization continues at a rapid pace – as the world population exceeds 7 billion and more than half is already living in towns and cities. Urban areas will face huge challenges in administration and planning, and resource demands could easily assume international dimensions. By some estimates, more and more conflicts will be fueled by resource gaps within countries, and failed cities as much as failed nation States.[8]

Multilateralism Beyond the Nation State

Box 3

Classically, multilateral institutions have existed to manage relationships among sovereign States. But globalization and technology have ushered in an era when more and more cross-border activity takes place outside the jurisdiction of the central State. A record number of migrants are on the move, nearly 215 million in 2010.[9] Over 1.5 billion people are now linked on social networks such as Facebook, both within and across countries and this number is expected to climb to 2.5 billion by 2016.[10] People in general are involved in patterns of "multilateral" communication that are not vertical and not within an institutional hierarchy, but that are nonetheless exerting a profound influence on societies, economies and politics – as the uprising in the Middle East and North Africa in 2011 made clear. For the most part, the State-centred multilateral system has yet to fully grasp these changes.

A new approach to multilateralism might emerge from the understanding that everyone is a stakeholder in it. In the era of globalization, everyone is affected by decisions made – or not made – in multilateral forums. The next step is to explore how to broker relationships that thread their way horizontally across borders and around States, and how these can lend systematic support to human rights and sustainable development.

Failing sustainable development

Many critiques of multilateralism have focused on the weaknesses and inefficiencies in its institutions, both those that serve as forums for political negotiations and those providing financing and development programming. Dissatisfaction with performance has prompted an escalating number of reform initiatives purporting to improve quality and effectiveness. After the first UN reform initiative was mooted in 1953, 14 more proposals were formulated until 1989. From 1990 to 2006, in less than half that time, 30 rounds of reform recommendations were put on the table.[11]

Is the UN reform debate framed too narrowly around "effectiveness"?

Most institutional reform discussions involve tinkering around the edges of the multilateral system, however, whether the issue is granting a few economically powerful developing countries a stronger role in governing the international financial institutions, or encouraging the UN development system to "deliver as one," an exercise so far focused more on realigning operational arrangements than on getting the broader policy framework right – and most importantly, getting the international trade and financial institutions and their national counter-parts in line with it.

If achieving human rights and the three pillars of sustainable development is the goal of multilateral engagement, the problems of multilateralism go far deeper. The sharp tip towards realpolitik has distorted multilateral debate and action. Gaps are growing unchecked on many fronts: between national and international decision-making, among the agendas of different national ministries, between commitments to sustainable development and progress in implementing them, between the emphasis on economic growth and real improvements in human well-being, between the need for resources and access to/control over them, and between the "rights" of capital and people's *human* rights.

Addressing the root causes of a multi-faceted record of failure

In an era of climate change and expanding social and economic disparities, there are clear global incentives for tipping the balance back towards principles, especially those of sustainable and inclusive development. But many States and institutions perpetuating the imbalance have benefited from the source of it – **an inequitable economic growth model**. Development has become increasingly unsustainable and unjust in many parts of the world, yet there is little room to meaningfully contest the current model or pursue alternatives. There is no multilateral mechanism strong enough to require a move towards sustainable development.

A consequence is that in the 20 years since the Rio Conference, threats to the well-being of people and the planet have escalated. Human rights and sustainable development imperatives such as essential services have been sidelined in favour of elite priorities such as short-term financial speculation and debt repayment. The **unsustainable consumption and production** patterns questioned at Rio have spread around the globe. **Biodiversity losses** have mounted, while **greenhouse gas emissions** continue to rise.

Billions of people remain poor and hungry because their economic and social rights, enshrined in binding multilateral agreements, has not been upheld and realized (see Box 4, page 23). In the area of **food**

insecurity, 20 years of deregulating commodities trading and allowing complex derivative products to flourish has transformed human nourishment – a basic and universal human right – into an economic asset. The value of food is traded in increasingly unstable and opaque commodities markets, even as one in six people in the world faces acute hunger.[12] Some financial speculators and industrial farms reap benefits; the majority of small farmers and consumers do not.

The **global decent work deficit** was already a "crisis before the crisis" in terms of mass unemployment, escalating inequalities not seen since the 1930s – and one of the contributory causes of the 2008 global financial crisis that triggered the Great Recession. Since the 1980s, when the current economic model began to be introduced worldwide, wage and income inequalities have increased in the majority of countries, with the share of income accruing to capital rising sharply, while wages and livelihood incomes have tended to stagnate or decline in both developed and developing countries.[13] In many countries, a combination of unregulated globalization and policy prescriptions delinked from human rights and sustainable development are on a collision course with the International Labour Organization's Decent Work Agenda.[14] Countries are required to compete based on which can provide the cheapest labour, or offer the loosest protections of workers' rights, or enact the lowest tax rates even when that drains domestic resources for improving productivity and labour conditions, or funding social protection.

A testament to the failure of the current economic-growth-only model is the recent finding that three-quarters of the world's poor people live in middle-income countries,[15] and that the middle-income country share of people in poverty has tripled in recent years,[16] regardless of measurement parameters. In other words, economies have grown, but the prospects for most people have not. The structural transformations required to equitably share the benefits of wealth creation and to balance progress across all three pillars of sustainable development are not being achieved, and likely will not be achieved without a multilateral system equipped for that end.

The "global" at the expense of the "local"

Behind the tensions between multilateralism and "policy space" mentioned earlier are the geographic or territorial imbalances underpinning the poor state of sustainability today. Namely: the prevailing policy framework has tended to favour the "global" – the global movement of goods and capital – at the expense of the "local" – policies aimed at nurturing and revitalizing local economies and societies, creating jobs where most people would like to stay if given a chance. For example a "favourable investment climate" is usually understood in mainstream policy circles as an enabling framework for foreign direct investments, even when certain rules can be at odds with the survival and development of the local economic fabric – the myriad small- and medium-sized enterprises and cooperatives that generate the bulk of employment worldwide.

Sub-national governments are at the forefront of this loss of "policy space" at the local level. They are often powerless in face of the widespread phenomenon of income concentration – when locally-generated wealth does not circulate locally in a virtuous cycle of local reinvestment and job creation, but instead gets "siphoned off" to financial centres (at home and abroad) to meet the ever higher short-term demands of finance-led globalization. Yet sub-national governments are among the least well represented stakeholders in multilateral processes that could tip the balance of policies, rules and regulations in favour of inclusive local development.

WOMEN PROTEST DEVELOPMENT
AID THAT STEALS THEIR LAND

Box 4

The following excerpt is from a letter from the League of Boeung Kak Women Struggling for Housing Rights to the World Bank President. It concerns a case of misdirected multilateral aid that, in being oriented mainly around elite interests, deepened existing injustices.

"We are the residents of Boeung Kak in Sras Choc commune, Phnom Penh, Cambodia who submitted a complaint to the World Bank Inspection Panel in September 2009. Our land rights, including our right to register our land, were unfairly denied by the World Bank-financed land-titling project. Instead our land has been leased to a private company and we are being forcibly evicted from our homes. We know that we have the right to be protected from forced eviction under the World Bank policy on involuntary resettlement. However, this policy is not being respected. ...

"In Cambodia today, land-grabbing by powerful people is increasing all the time. ... We are losing our land, our homes and our livelihoods. Our children are forced to drop out of school. We have no food security and our mental health is deteriorating. We cannot find justice at the courts, which only work for the rich and the powerful. When we try to protest, we are threatened, arrested, beaten and abused.

"Every year, [Cambodia] receives more than one billion dollars in aid and loans from international banks and donors. But much of this aid is not reaching the poor. ... We believe that the donors are a part of our problem when they fail to monitor their aid to ensure that it does not cause harm.

"In Boeung Kak, ... [f]or the past four years we have been living under the threat of forced eviction. In the last two years more than 2,000 families in our neighborhood have already been evicted. We have been intimidated by company security forces and local authorities, and we are concerned about our personal security. They threaten that our homes will be burned if we do not move. Our homes have been flooded by the company with sewage water and some have even been buried in sand. Even though we are the rightful owners of our homes and land, we have only been offered a small fraction of the market price. This is not enough for us to buy another house in the city. ...

"We have proposed a solution to this dispute. We are willing to share our land with the developer if the government will build us new housing onsite. We have asked the municipality of Phnom Penh to reserve 12 percent of the leased area for this purpose. We have also asked the World Bank to support the government to make this plan possible. ...

"We call for accountability, not just for our Boeung Kak community, but for all the people suffering from land-grabbing and forced evictions throughout Cambodia. Justice for Boeung Kak is justice for all Cambodians!"

Source: Bretton Woods Project [www.brettonwoodsproject.org/art-567912]

Three fault-lines: decisions, implementation, institutions

The weaknesses in today's multilateral system operate along at least three major fault-lines:

- The poor quality of decision-making;

- The poor record of implementation;

- The ongoing fragmentation of multilateral institutions.

Poor quality of decision-making

The poor quality of decision-making stems in large part from a lack of inclusiveness, or democratic deficit. A narrowing definition of what multilateral engagement should aim to accomplish has fostered participation based on "pay to play." Governments of wealthier countries have a louder voice, as do the international financial institutions, civil society groups from developed countries, and activists from urban areas and socioeconomically privileged communities.

There is an implicit assumption that multilateral participation involves different groups sitting around a table, with far less emphasis on considering all perspectives and sources of evidence, or on ensuring buy-in so that all participants have a meaningful stake in working to achieve what ends up being agreed. This hinders people's right to participate in choices that affect them, and makes decisions more limited in scope and ambition.

The executive branches of government and individual ministries (particularly finance and trade) have come to dominate positions in multilateral discussions within all-important economic forums. This further reinforces a "special interest" approach that misses, or limits the potentially valuable contributions of other ministries and stakeholders, such as legislatures and sub-national governments, or representatives of constituencies directly affected by the decisions taken. Among poorer developing countries, additional constraints come from the gaps in financial and technical resources that continue to undercut their abilities to negotiate with more powerful players.

Poor record of implementation

A second fault-line in the multilateral system is the poor record of implementing international commitments to human rights and sustainable development. Again, inequities and double-standards are a major underlying cause.

Inconsistencies and contradictions include the unstated assumption that less powerful nations have a greater burden than more powerful ones to implement what has been decided, despite the internationally agreed principle of common but differentiated responsibility, and with far greater scrutiny of their implementation record than is true for more powerful States.

As mentioned earlier, both middle-income and poorer States face prescriptions and constraints on the space they have to make domestic policy choices consistent with sustainable development. They may be called on to prioritize attracting short-term foreign investment flows over cultivating domestic industries that over the long term can provide decent jobs and a stronger tax base. They may be required to purchase technology or hire experts from foreign companies instead of building capacities to develop or produce their own. These choices often involve splitting human rights and the three dimensions of sustainable development from each other, resulting in public policies that are contradictory and incoherent.

Incoherence is fostered by the continued heavy reliance, in multilateral and other forums, on measurements that do not capture all dimensions of sustainable development, and that fail to factor in costs such as environmental damages. These produce an incomplete picture of the issues at stake. They not only hinder the formulation of responses consistent with human rights and sustainable development, but also serve to justify prevailing economic models. Some multilateral reform initiatives have advocated measuring the results of development programmes and policies to prove their "effectiveness," but with a reductionist turn, where actions are pursued because they can be measured, not because they can bring about the transformation that human rights and sustainable development require.

Poor progress on sustainable development also stems from more limited multilateral commitments, with one prominent example being the Millennium Development Goals (MDGs). Called a kind of lowest common denominator for development, these are oriented mainly around improved service delivery to achieve a set of targets and indicators, but not around reconfiguring the skewed systems of production and consumption that generate gaps in services to start with.

The MDGs in fact reveal the political dynamics that led to their selection. They have targets and indicators for development goals such as poverty reduction, but not for the "global partnerships" that are supposed to help achieve these. International development assistance does have a longstanding internationally agreed target for quantity, but this has never been reached, and does not address a number of quality concerns, such as aid tied to procurement in source countries. About half of bilateral assistance from members of the Development Assistance Committee (DAC) of the Organisation for Economic Co-operation and Development (OECD) never reaches developing countries at all.[17] Less than a third of official development assistance goes through the multilateral system.[18]

Ongoing fragmentation of multilateral institutions

A third fault-line in multilateralism involves the ongoing fragmentation of multilateral institutions. This extends to a more significant level than the one commonly associated with the "One UN" reform and coordination discussions. The fact that there is still no clear accountability of the WTO and the international financial institutions to the UN's human rights and sustainable development prerogatives has consistently diminished prospects for coherent action. The most well-resourced parts of the multilateral system, namely the IMF and World Bank, continue to advocate unsustainable economic models – almost half of World Bank lending related to energy involves finite and climate-damaging fossil fuels, for example.[19] The thrust of WTO negotiations continue to prioritize trade liberalization even when it may clash with sustainable development considerations, such as full and decent employment, food security and the balanced use of environmental resources. The UN, which produced the commitments to sustainable development, has become a place mainly to monitor and discuss issues. It lacks the resources or political weight to go very far in backing the implementation of commitments.

Gaps in institutional frameworks and regulations are also fuelling unsustainability and human rights regressions. There is still no legal framework for a country to restructure its debt, for example, even though this process is critical to public budgeting. Debt restructuring for developing countries remains moderated by the Paris Club, an informal group of 19 wealthy nations that operates outside the multilateral system with no accountability except to its members, and without multilaterally endorsed responsible lending and borrowing criteria. There is no international cooperation around or oversight over taxation to end the "race to the bottom" that occurs through cutting taxes to compete for foreign investment. Despite the global financial crisis, no serious breakthrough is in sight for the creation of a new international reserve system necessary to prevent future financial crises stemming from global imbalances and asymmetric adjustments between trade surplus and deficit countries. Many transnational business activities occur untaxed and unregulated by either national or international laws, with no safeguards in place to protect against sudden and destabilizing draw-downs of foreign investment.

Special Focus: Questioning Some Terms of Debate

Breaking the impasse in multilateralism requires engaging in an open debate, drawing on the perspectives of all stakeholders, around what kinds of development and governance models the multilateral system should be endorsing, how it can be responsive to the sustainable development priorities of countries operating in highly diverse circumstances, who needs to make which contributions to accomplish sustainable development for the world at large, and what should be measured to assess that achievement. A series of questions could move this debate forward, particularly on four core issues:

- Effectiveness;
- Representation;
- Accountability; and
- Neutrality.

Effectiveness

No one would dispute the value of effectiveness. But the term is often narrowly applied in multilateral debates, linked to operational mechanics rather than substantive issues. A broader perspective might come from asking:

1. How is effectiveness defined, and what is its focus?

2. What does it mean to view effectiveness in terms of social, economic, political and environmental systems, not just discrete projects and sectors, and tie it more closely to achieving human rights and sustainable development objectives?

3. What are the impacts on effectiveness of limited policy space and contradictory standards for different sectors of sustainable development?

4. How and by whom are results defined, and what happens when they are primarily defined by funding sources?

5. How should effectiveness be measured, and using what indicators?

6. Are current indicators capturing dimensions of development besides production and income? Can they assess effectiveness if they do not reflect gains and gaps in human rights; the equitable distribution of assets, environmental resources, jobs and other sustainable development fundamentals; and social and environmental costs?

7. Where effectiveness requires transformation, how do we move beyond vested interests and tendencies to tinker at the margins? Are there any configurations of stakeholders who have managed to do this?

Representation

Wider participation in the multilateral system has been endorsed, but the quality of representation, whether in terms of issues raised or the voices being heard, has received less emphasis. A different approach to defining quality representation might come from asking:

1. Who should be at the multilateral table and what attributes should they possess?

2. Who should represent a country? Should representation draw more consistently from ministries outside those of finance and

foreign affairs, as well as parliaments, sub-national governments and civil society? Would this change the nature of the multilateral agenda?[20]

3. Can decision-making be framed by the imperative of policy coherence, so that decisions in one arena do not contradict those made in another, and all decisions contribute to (and do not undermine) progress on human rights and sustainable development?

4. Are democratic deficits at the national level being translated into democratic deficits in the multilateral system, and if so, how can these be corrected?

5. If multilateral decision-making reflects deepening inequities in the world, how can the balance be tipped back towards a broader representation of interests and more comprehensive debates?

6. How can minority voices be better heard in the process of reaching international consensus?

7. Should high-quality, globally representative institutions be viewed as a global public good that should be equipped to consistently act on behalf of collective interests?

Accountability

One result of the dominance of realpolitik in the multilateral system is skewed accountability. The more powerful have made themselves less accountable, and have reduced the definition of accountability to fit their interests, so that it becomes more about how money is spent, for example, than the quality of contributions to human rights and sustainable development. This limited vision might be challenged by asking:

1. Who is accountable for upholding the principles of human rights and sustainable development? To whom are these actors accountable?

2. Is accountability consistently upheld across making, implementing and monitoring multilateral decisions? If not, what are the gaps in accountability, and what impacts do they have?

3. Is there a tendency for those with less capacity to uphold human rights and attain sustainable development to be held more accountable for achieving them? If so, how can that imbalance be rectified?

4. Should accountability imply the willingness to step back from individual national interests when the collective good requires doing so?

5. Do accountability mechanisms need to be reconfigured to go beyond efficiency and effectiveness in spending funds to support more ambitious aspirations and actions? How can informed risk-taking and constructive failure be factored into accountability, so that accountability allows for innovation and becomes about more than just compliance with an existing set of rules and/or predefined results and outcomes?

6. What kinds of multilateral governance structures and resource flows best support accountability for human rights and sustainable development?

7. Should systems of accountability aim to cover the greater array of stakeholders now active in multilateralism? Should accountability include broadening space for minority perspectives that are not being heard?

8. Does the current UN human rights accountability framework, primarily based on State obligations within the nation's territory, fail to adequately hold States to account for the transnational impact of their policies both unilaterally and through collective decision-making in multilateral institutions?

Neutrality

The multilateral system was founded on the principle of neutrality, but this notion is often broadly and simplistically applied. Deconstructing it for a closer look involves asking:

1. How can notions of neutrality be rooted in the reality that the founding principles of the UN are not neutral, but the process of achieving them can be? Can that process enable diverse stakeholders to find their own paths towards human rights and sustainable development?

2. Is neutrality as a kind of lowest common denominator being used to limit aspirations of multilateralism?

3. What happens to multilateral neutrality when some countries exempt themselves from international standards? What are the implications for sustainable development and human rights?

4. What biases enter the process of implementing and monitoring globally agreed standards? To what extent are factors such as funding patterns, different degrees of political voice and variable expectations around accountability driving these biases?

5. How is neutrality weakened by the ongoing emphasis on income-based growth and the lack of coherence across international agreements?

What If:
Aspirations for the Future of Multilateralism

The final chapter of this book presents a series of recommendations for reforming the current multilateral system. But first, this section aims higher. It puts aside the constraints of the current system to examine what an equitable model of multilateralism might look like, premised on the notion of rights and sustainability, and empowered to balance and regulate the political, economic and social shifts brought by globalization.

The essence of this system would be a new, Geneva Convention-style set of international laws and standards to manage the transnational impacts of all activities related to human rights and sustainable development, including trade and investment patterns, tax and employment policies, the reserve currency system, safe migration and the stewardship of environmental resources. These standards would carry legal and moral force, thereby empowering the multilateral system to lead in cultivating collective global responsibility and ownership.

> WHAT COULD AN EQUITABLE MODEL OF MULTILATERALISM LOOK LIKE, BASED ON THE NOTION OF RIGHTS AND SUSTAINABILITY?

The following pages look at elements of such a framework in four areas – sustainable development and human rights, representation and decision-making, measurement and institutional reform.

First, all multilateral actions should be guided by the principles of sustainable development and human rights

There is now a comprehensive body of international agreements, starting with the UN Charter, that elaborate and commit to human rights and sustainable development principles, both in general and for specific aspects of development, from gender equality to water rights to the rights of indigenous peoples. Many of these have been translated into national legal frameworks.

If these principles became the conceptual foundation for multilateralism and were put in practice, all multilateral decisions, programmes, resources, indicators for measurement and accountability mechanisms would have to correspond accordingly. The multilateral system would be oriented around equity and inclusiveness, and achieving human rights and sustainable development. These principles would equally apply to areas including macroeconomic and development frameworks, financial regulations, trade, international law, peace and security, and choices to address climate change. Human rights would be upheld through all actions by the multilateral system, and multilateral agreements on rights would extend to include the rights of the planet to be protected for its future well-being and that of its human inhabitants.

Applying the right to water, for example, then would become about making sure that everyone has access to adequate, quality supplies at an affordable cost. There could be different means to attain this end. The most effective strategy would depend on working within local circumstances to achieve this right, rather than on one-size-fits-all prescriptions. Further, since the right to water could be presumed to extend to future generations, the provision of water would need to fully factor in potential external costs, such as from environmental damages. It would need to take into account that nature has "rights" to have resources treated in a manner that ensures their longevity and ability to sustain all forms of life.

Applying human rights and sustainable development principles to economic and development strategies means they would need to move beyond the incremental and aim for systemic transformation. The multilateral system would advocate macroeconomic policies that prioritize the promotion of decent work. There would be agreement on and implementation of a global, purchasing-power-adjusted minimum wage, rather than just a poverty line, so that people could be assured of a basic income, and countries would not be forced to cut wages below a certain level to compete for foreign investments. The systems of trade and investment rules would be overhauled and regulated to provide the industries, jobs and services that people need for sustainable development, while a new international reserve currency system would be in place oriented around similar aims. Consumption and production patterns would be managed based on the sustainable development needs of a given population and linked to an equitable balance of per capita greenhouse gas emissions.

All forms of external financing for development would be directed towards achieving sustainable development and human rights. Criteria for fair and responsible lending [as well as borrowing] would guide loans made by multilateral banks as well as debt workout mechanisms, and both debtors and creditors would be fairly represented in related systems of governance and decision-making.

Official development assistance would be pooled in one "multilateral fund" so that it would remain disconnected from other priorities such as favouring interests in countries where aid originates. Administered by a diverse and regionally representative group of States, including those who are recipients of ODA, it would be directed towards achieving human rights and sustainable development outcomes, not towards policy conditionalities dictating how those outcomes should be reached. New systems of data collection and sharing would do more to link global and national actions, including by better defining sustainable development needs and priorities, as well as access to resources, expertise and technology. The countries and sub-national regions with the greatest needs and most limited capacities would be prioritized for support.

Second, global decision-making should aspire to a broader vision

A broader vision of multilateral decision-making would entail a rebalancing of pragmatism and principles in multilateral forums that is in line with sustainable development and the global collective good. Governments would endorse a concept of national sovereignty that is rooted not just in the pursuit of national interest, but in the collective interest of all peoples and countries – where for instance, international action would be taken to reign in financial markets, thereby expanding policy space and democratic sovereignty at the national level.

Since multilateral decision-making would be valued as the only avenue broad enough to manage all the interconnected steps towards achieving human rights and sustainable development, all States would have an incentive to support strong multilateral decisions as more effective in some cases than those rooted in unilateral dominance. The balance of national and collective good would foster understanding of the moral imperatives of sustainable development, human rights and equity, along with the practical benefits of living in a world where broadly shared prosperity maintains security and stability, and where the environment is managed in a way that sustains human life now and for generations to come.

There would be strong emphasis on closing the implementation gap that stems from making multilateral agreements and not putting them into practice. All agreements, while setting standards, would also outline a strategy for implementation and resource allocation. New and emerging sustainable development and human rights concerns – especially those posing the greatest threats to global public goods – would require legally binding and enforceable international conventions.

Political decision-makers would accept the challenge of setting a high bar for political consensus, rather than the lowest common denominator, while recognizing that equity and inclusion considerations may require new kinds of flexibilities in how agreed standards are achieved. The principle of non-discrimination – where all parties are equal before the law, which can solidify inequalities and historical disadvantages – would be understood as non-discrimination in the ability to accomplish sustainable development outcomes. This would require affirmative action measures for States and peoples who have insufficient resources and capacities. Applying the principle of non-discrimination would reinforce grounds for invalidating multilateral decisions that contradict international or national human rights and sustainable development objectives.

Finally, bringing new perspectives and leadership into decision-making would produce new thinking about the blocs of countries participating in multilateral negotiations. New alliances would be forged around common human rights and sustainable development priorities rather than more conventional alignments related to region or economic size. States, particularly those that otherwise would have little voice, would operate from a stronger collective bargaining position. Room for nations that continue to promote unsustainable practices would shrink.

Third, achieving sustainable development and human rights should drive the reform of multilateral institutions

Most current discussions about reforming multilateral institutions focus on achieving better "results" through new systems of management, better coordination, tighter auditing and evaluation procedures, and so on. Or they emphasize increasing seats on governance boards. But these initiatives do not address the ways in which the multilateral system is fundamentally misaligned with the objective of achieving human rights and sustainable development. If institutional reform considered multilateral institutions in light of these objectives, it would start by asking which infrastructure, resources and capacities would need to be in place to fully support nations in reaching those ends.

This approach to institutional reform would shift the hierarchy of priorities in the multilateral system, bringing sustainable development and human rights concerns to the top in terms of how institutions are established, funded and governed. Institutions would be regrouped under more holistic mandates based on achieving human rights and sustainable development outcomes, so that, for example, they would support nations to develop and implement strategies to reduce inequalities and disparities, not just to expedite aggregate economic growth.

All multilateral institutions would be required to routinely engage with each other in order to offer coherent multilateral support for human rights and sustainable development. Loan agreements by financial institutions would be reviewed by development agencies, which would weigh in on proposals affecting public budgets for health, education, employment creation and so on. All proposed multilateral development initiatives, including loans and country level development programmes, would also entail reviews by affected stakeholders, and multilateral institutions would be required to respond and justify positions that have been questioned.

Rather than relying on voluntary funding for core development institutions, the multilateral system would define minimum budgets funded by assessed contributions from States based on their financial capabilities. Additional voluntary funds could also be provided, but they would go into a single pool of funds within each agency, and reporting on fund use would be done through the executive board, not to individual donors. Over time, more thought would go into which situations require multilateral institutions to support progress towards human rights and sustainable development, and which might benefit from other arrangements.

Fourth, measures of development progress must include sustainability, equity and human rights

The limited scope of measurements of development progress used to analyze progress and to make multilateral decisions has undercut prospects for sustainable development – and the effectiveness of multilateralism – by focusing debate primarily on reducing poverty, and increasing economic production and consumption (standard of living). More complete, integrated measures would uphold sustainable development principles in their conception, design and use. They would tell the entire story of what is needed to achieve social progress, sustainable development and human rights, and monitor whether or not these objectives are being achieved.

These new measurements of progress would be based on the premise that human rights and sustainable development are global objectives, and cover all actions with international impact – including from national economic policies. They would be designed to integrate markers of human rights, and social, economic and environmental progress as part of aiming for the systemic and holistic transformation that sustainable development implies. As such, they would improve the quality of decisions, support consistency in policy choices and bolster accountability.

They would also close a number of gaps. First, measures of human well-being would expand beyond income averages and aggregate GDP to reflect the distribution of income, and non-market activities, such as household labour, including by capturing gender and age-based differences in time use. New measures would incorporate costs from economic growth, such as damages to the environment or the deprivations of poverty-wage jobs, as well as costs from not acting on a given issue, such as productivity losses when people cannot access health care.

Objective and subjective measures of well-being would be identified in order to assess inequalities. By linking various dimensions of the quality of life, these would shed light on the consequences of people facing multiple forms of discrimination, including through gender, ethnicity and location.[21] They would explore whether and how inequality affects development and human rights, and consider the impact of redistributive policies such as land reform, progressive taxation, employment guarantees and social protection.[22]

Second, better measures would be interlinked, in order to indicate whether or not people can realize their rights. Nutritional measures would show how many people have an adequate diet, but would be linked to measures of their ability to access healthy food, such as the practice of feeding boys before girls. Indicators for livelihoods would make the link to property rights, especially for women, who often cannot realize this right under the law or through custom. Human rights measures overall would improve through the development of methodologies for more concretely measuring the fulfillment of rights, through a greater focus on State obligations and not just individual enjoyment of rights, and through greater accuracy in measuring the progressive realization of rights over time.[23]

To fill a third gap, new measures would integrate economic as well as environmental sustainability, tracking what is happening now while factoring in what can reasonably be predicted for the future. They would weigh the mid-to-long-term costs of encouraging foreign investments that limit the development of domestic industrial capacities, for example, or that produce jobs with wages so low that parents cannot afford to send a future generation of children to school. They could encourage not just a push for manufacturing, but for industrial development along a low-carbon path defined by regular ratings of carbon consumption. Consumption and production patterns as a whole would be measured for a balance that considers human well-being and the health of ecological resources. For countries and people that are currently over-consuming resources, new measures would tie aggregate consumption cuts to more equitable and sustainable resource use.

Pragmatism and Principles: Recommended Actions for Now

So far, this publication has explored the current state of multi-lateralism, and how in the future it could do more to advance human rights and sustainable development. Many challenges stand in the way of change, yet debates are flourishing around what improvements need to be made. There is growing recognition, in diverse quarters, that current imbalances in the patterns of globalization and the multilateral responses to them are unjust and contrary to common interests.

> MANY CHALLENGES STAND IN THE WAY OF CHANGE, YET DEBATES ARE FLOURISHING AROUND WHAT IMPROVEMENTS NEED TO BE MADE.

Poor quality results for rights and sustainability have spurred many calls for increased international regulation, adherence to global treaties and rights instruments, new global governance bodies, broader accountability mechanisms, new financial mechanisms such as a global financial transaction tax, and the strengthening of institutions engaged in monitoring and implementing international commitments.

The following recommendations will not take the multilateral system all the way to where it needs to be. But they do comprise proposals that are a beginning, that are actionable and that may spark other ideas. Some are primarily the responsibility of different levels of governments and multilateral institutions. All can be propelled by the advocacy of civil society and social movements. None of them require a change in the UN Charter. They are grouped under six dimensions of a multilateralism equipped to do much more to attain equitable sustainable development.

Aim high to restore aspirations, and rebalance pragmatism and principles

- Develop new mechanisms within the Human Rights Council to **hold States accountable for the transboundary human rights impact of their policies**, whether resulting from unilateral measures or the positions taken in multilateral institutions, especially the WTO, international financial institutions, and regional bodies.

- Adopt a **new Charter on the Right to Sustainable Development**, which should emphasize the commitment of governments to policy coherence for human rights and sustainability. It should reconfirm the obligation to the progressive realization of human rights using the maximum available resources and expand it to the right to sustainable development and the rights of future generations. It should acknowledge the concept of planetary boundaries. It should confirm the principle of fair burden sharing and equitable per capita rights towards the global commons and to the emission of greenhouse gases, taking fully into account the historical responsibilities of societies.

- Create a new council integrating the three pillars of sustainable development. The **Council on Sustainable Development** would be mandated to achieve two of the UN Charter's four foundational objectives (human rights, and economic and social progress), and make significant contributions to the other two (security and international law). Convening less than the full number of UN Member States at a given time, it would have rotating, constituency-based representation across States that are diverse in terms of size, location and economic strength. One constituency should be States that have made contributions to human rights and sustainable development, in accordance with internationally agreed standards and national baselines. Council membership would need to reflect the positions of effective national counterparts and placed in an influential governance position vis-à-vis other ministries and interests. The council's jurisdiction would extend to all multilateral bodies, including the international financial institutions. The new council would be charged with overseeing the reporting process for implementing the new Charter on the Right to Sustainable Development.

- To strengthen well-being and equity, define and implement a **universal social protection floor**. It would uphold all three pillars of sustainable development through income guarantees, minimum social services and sustainable environmental measures. Link this concept to multilateral policies and programmes to support implementation and financing, under the principle of common but differentiated responsibility, so that countries that cannot afford social protection floors receive support from those that can.

- Mobilize a worldwide campaign to **promote global citizenship**, and raise popular awareness of and expectations for human rights and sustainable development. The campaign should explain, in accessible terms, why trade, finance, macroeconomics, human rights, environmental issues and social sectors are interlinked. It should emphasize how considering these issues in combination, guided by human rights and sustainable development principles, can improve the quality of development choices and the lives of most people.

SETTING AN EXAMPLE

Box 5

Some countries have taken steps to make sustainable development part of national laws. In 2011, Bolivia passed the first laws granting nature rights equal to those of people. Eleven rights will include those to life, to vital cycles without human alteration, and to freedom from pollution. Nature will be protected from any infrastructure and development projects that affect the balance of ecosystems or local inhabitants.

Bolivia has suffered a history of environmental degradation mainly due to mining. Setting a new direction may be difficult, however, because a third of the country's foreign currency still comes from the mining industry.

Ecuador has changed its Constitution to give rights to nature, although oil companies continue to destroy biologically rich areas of the Amazon within its territory.

Both Bolivia and Ecuador make reference to the concept of *buen vivir* (good living) in their Constitutions. *Buen vivir* is a kind of holistic life philosophy that draws on the worldview of indigenous peoples in the Andes region. It allows all members of a society to pursue material, social and spiritual satisfaction, but not if that harms other people or the natural world.

The concept does not imply negating social modernization of society and the value of technology. But it does break from a solely materialistic notion of wealth. Ecuadorian economist Alberto Acosta, a former Energy Minister and President of the Constituent Assembly, underlines the human rights claim on the state inherent in buen vivir in stating: "All individuals enjoy the same right to a life in dignity encompassing health, food, shelter, a healthy environment, education, a livelihood, recreation and social security."

Further, nature could be seen as possessing rights because it is freed from a designation as solely an object of property.

Source: 11 April, Guardian, John Vidal, "In Search of Buen Vivir" 2010

Make participation meaningful

- Where multilateral decision-making is better served through involving a more limited number of participants, **require all categories of countries to be equally represented**. Global economic governance, for example, would include not only the most powerful countries, but also representatives from the least-developed countries and smaller middle-income countries.

- In the face of geopolitical stalemates, work towards a **new, fluid political configuration of temporary groupings** of UN Member States based on commitment to sustainable development and human rights, and oriented around strengthening the quality of processes and results.

- Require secretariats of multilateral institutions to **inform national legislatures and interested sub-national bodies** of all multilateral decision-making processes, including by providing preliminary materials and outcomes. This would entail active communications, moving beyond static web postings to involve regular contacts with parliamentary sub-committees and canvassing of sub-national authorities for subjects most relevant to them.

- To further harness expertise that supports more substantive, better quality political decision-making, require multilateral secretariats to **set up and moderate online forums for diverse stakeholders** – such as technical experts in and outside the multilateral system, civil society groups and people affected by the issues under discussion – that are **linked to specific political negotiations and policy decisions** guiding the multilateral system. Secretariats would draw on the forums for evidence to set agendas, and integrate relevant information and analysis in draft negotiating texts considered by governments. Final draft agreements would be circulated through the forums to test their quality, including by screening for negative consequences for human rights or sustainable development, and towards engaging stakeholders in implementing and monitoring decisions. Based on the many good practices at national and sub-national levels, draft agreements would also be subject to a mandatory public comment stage. Serious gaps in final decisions could be raised before the council on sustainable development, or appealed under a high-level body on policy coherence, as described in the recommendations below.

- To help build a broader global constituency for effective multilateralism, and deepen public ownership in the outcomes of multilateral decisions, post all draft multilateral resolutions on the Internet and **actively solicit global public feedback**, including through social media. Compile useful ideas for consideration by relevant stakeholder forums and multilateral political negotiations.

- To strengthen national priorities in the global arena, advocate for **quality national representation** by both developed and developing countries, so that representatives in multilateral forums are not only foreign service and finance and trade ministry officials, but are also experts from other sectors, sub-national officials and other stakeholders. They should be equipped to make meaningful contributions to achieving human rights and sustainable development.

- Give space for civil society processes to develop their own mechanisms of constituency and regional representation and enable their representatives to participate on a par with governments in drafting committees, along the lines of the Food and Agriculture Organization of the United Nations (FAO) framework (see Box 6).

CIVIL SOCIETY MECHANISM OF THE COMMITTEE ON WORLD FOOD SECURITY

Box 6

In 2009, the Committee on World Food Security (CFS) underwent a reform process that, among others, led to the creation of the Civil Society Mechanism (CSM). The CSM is an autonomous mechanism – fully set-up and built by civil society – that provides an inclusive space for dialogue and for debating varying positions among a wide range of civil society organizations, with the ultimate goal to find common positions to present to the CFS. The governing body of the CSM is the Coordination Committee, which has the responsibility to facilitate civil society participation in the CFS, including in negotiation and decision-making. Its members are chosen through a sophisticated election process from among 11 constituencies (farmers; fisherfolk; indigenous peoples; herders/pastoralists; landless peoples; youth; consumers; urban poor; women; NGOs; and agriculture and food workers) and 16 sub-regions.

Representatives of the CSM can actively participate on a par with government delegates in the drafting process of decisions and policies to address food insecurity and sometimes they can help broker consensus when opinions differ. They do not have voting power – as this remains with governments – but as the CFS mainly operates through consensus building, they do not necessarily need to have voting power to influence the negotiation and decision-making process.

Insist on policy coherence

- Establish a political body at the highest level, such as a refocused General Assembly, that would uphold the consistent orientation of public policies around the achievement of human rights and sustainable development: a General Assembly **high level body on policy coherence**. Cases of policy incoherence stemming from both the public and private sectors – such as when one multilateral organization advocates carbon-intensive growth and another promotes low-carbon development, or when trade priorities trump decent labour – could be adjudicated, including through legal processes. To help uphold the integrity of decisions in multilateral forums, the body would also consider cases where individual countries, groups of States, multilateral institutions or civil society could contest undue pressure to compromise policy coherence. The body would offer a final arbitration mechanism for protecting domestic policy space to achieve human rights and sustainable development from external interference, including as related to trade and financing for development, as well as all other issues considered in multilateral forums.

- Mandate the **new Sustainable Development Council to review all recommendations of its own Universal Periodic Review mechanism** (see Box 7 and section below), and to define and monitor how the multilateral system can link programmes, policies and financing to support human rights and sustainable development.

- **Fill global regulatory gaps** that undermine sustainable development and human rights, including those on financial speculation, sovereign debt workouts, taxation, private sector entities that are "too big to fail," and pollution and consumption patterns, among others. Regulations should be oriented towards global and national level actions (see also "Bretton Woods II").

- Recognizing that national and global priorities are increasingly intertwined, **address gaps between national and international governance** so that national policy coherence fully aligns with global policy coherence to support sustainable development and human rights. Each country can consider appropriate mechanisms, backed by adequate resources and political clout. Examples could include an ombudsperson function, a policy Sherpa or a parliamentary committee dedicated to coherence.

- **Hold a United Nations "Bretton Woods II"** Conference on Financial and Monetary Reforms, to agree on implementation of the major recommendations of the "Stiglitz Commission" to address the many systemic risks still underpinning the global financial and monetary system, and reforms needed to redirect finance to human rights and sustainability goals.

- Undertake an open, transparent and participatory process to **review provisions in multilateral, regional and bilateral**

trade and investment agreements that give undue protection of the rights of foreign investors and may prevent introduction of new policies and regulations to support human rights and sustainable development objectives – including in relation to local employment and enterprise development, technology transfer, health and environmental protection. **Agree on the primacy of food security and livelihoods** of small farmers and indigenous peoples over tariff reduction commitments taken in trade agreements.

Box 7

THE UNIVERSAL PERIODIC REVIEW

In 2006, a new multilateral mechanism was created to review the records of UN Member States in upholding human rights. The Universal Periodic Review operates under the auspices of the UN Human Rights Council. At least one in every four years, each of the 193 UN Member States submits a comprehensive report on actions to protect and advance human rights.

By being universal, the review ensures that all countries are considered under the same standards. All Member States were expected to report at least once by the end of 2011.

Implement internationally agreed principles

- The new **Sustainable Development Council should be equipped with its own Universal Periodic Review mechanism** similar to the one established with the Human Rights Council (see Box 7, page 55), so that all countries report on measures to achieve sustainable development, covering all relevant issues linked to human rights, trade, macroeconomic policy, the environment, financing and political participation. The UPR concept should be enhanced to consider information provided not only by governments, but also by other stakeholders, such as civil society and the private sector. Information on reports and Universal Periodic Review findings would be made widely available through information channels that actively target all relevant stakeholders.

- **Reorient economic analysis, research and reporting by multilateral institutions** to include the impact of any activities on advancing human rights and all three pillars of sustainable development, factoring in the impacts of cross-border activities; and proactively inform parliamentarians and the public about their findings.

- **Develop markers to track the financing and implementation of activities** to achieve human rights and the three pillars of sustainable development. Require multilateral institutions to use the markers, and foster their application elsewhere. Widely disseminate data from the markers and encourage their use in advocacy by civil society groups, multilateral institutions, parliamentarians and other stakeholders.

- **Apply the principle of mutual accountability** in framing public external financing agreements, including for loans and grants, to achieve human rights and sustainable development. Move the traditional donor-recipient relationship towards a contractual approach, where each party is understood to have obligations that, if unfulfilled, nullify the contract. Agreements would stipulate that all parties would apply human rights and sustainable development principles, whether they are giving or receiving funds.

- Across all efforts to advance human rights and sustainable development, move towards implementation models that **fully build on and value contributions from stakeholders**. Call on those with more capacities and resources, financial or otherwise, to assume a greater responsibility to carry implementation forward, but primarily through a process of partnership that systematically fosters balanced and meaningful participation. Design monitoring and evaluation tools to measure the quality and diversity of stakeholder engagement, and use them to guide present and future plans and programmes.

- **Monitor and revise procurement policies**, whether domestic or trans-border, to align with sustainable development priorities such as the creation of decent jobs, the development of manufacturing and technology capacities for marginalized countries and people, and environmental protection.

- Support stronger domestic tax capacities, and work towards ending tax evasion. **Establish an intergovernmental UN Tax Committee** as the first international body for cooperation on tax policy, towards setting standards that would reduce tax competition and ensure the availability of resources for social protection, decent employment, economic diversification and other aspects of sustainable development.

- **Create a global mechanism/fund for technology** that poorer countries can use to support domestic development, incubation and manufacturing of technologies to support a healthy economy, create decent jobs or protect the environment. Mandate this to assess the value of technology using the precautionary and other core sustainable development principles. Establish a separate arbitration mechanism to moderate related disputes.

Reinvent the reform discussion

- Require **all multilateral institutions to have an internationally agreed normative basis** for their operations that supports policy coherence, and is reflected in their programmes, monitoring and governance. Where necessary, uphold accountability through the high-level body on policy coherence.

- Establish measures **to make the work of the international financial institutions and WTO more coherent with that of the UN**, including through required institutional audits, monitoring and evaluation, and a universal mandate review that for each organization assesses the consistency of support for human rights and all three pillars of sustainable development.

- **Reduce the dependence of UN development activities on ODA funding**, starting with agreement on alternatives such as a global financial transaction tax.

- **Develop a form of regional multilateralism that is truly supportive of human rights and sustainable development.** Regional financial and monetary arrangements (such as regional development banks, reserve pooling and complementary currencies or payment systems for intra-regional trade) must provide genuine alternatives to existing global and regional financial institutions – whether in terms of their guiding development models, investment principles and safeguards, and governance modalities. Regional financial and monetary cooperation and macroeconomic coordination should as much as possible serve to enhance policy space for measures tailored to local conditions and needs through enhanced protection against the policy dictates of financial markets.

Make measurement meaningful

- Wherever applicable, ensure that all measurements linked to sustainable development reflect **dimensions of distribution and equity**, including as they extend over different and future generations.

- **Recognize that not everything of value can be measured.** Question the growing tendency to impose results-based management and similar systems, which is focusing too much attention on what can be measured, rather than on what needs to be done. Conduct research on measurement alternatives for qualitative achievements, and advocate that foreign aid donors in particular reexamine their approaches to this issue.

- Towards advocating for more meaningful measurement **in the Beyond 2015 process, build on existing initiatives seeking** to expand the scope of measurements, such as the work of the Stiglitz-Sen-Fitoussi Commission, the "happiness" resolution submitted to the General Assembly by Bhutan and 60 co-sponsor Member States (see Box 8), and the Greenhouse Development Rights Framework built around the concept of "comparability of effort." The framework combines a measure of responsibility (including historic contributions to greenhouse gas pollution, excluding emissions associated with meeting basic necessities) with a measure of capacity (broadly, the ability to pay without sacrificing necessities), with both defined in a manner sensitive to inequalities within countries.

- **Hold a summit level meeting to agree on new international standards for assessing sustainable development.** It would define the elements of a new metric that would replace GDP, reflect multilateral principles and commitments across the three pillars, capture income and non-income dimensions, and end the externalization of costs.

BOX 8

HAPPINESS: A HOLISTIC APPROACH TO DEVELOPMENT

General Assembly Resolution A/65/L.86, "Happiness: towards a holistic approach to development" states:

Recognizing that the gross domestic product indicator by nature was not designed to and does not adequately reflect the happiness and well-being of people in a country,

Conscious that unsustainable patterns of production and consumption can impede sustainable development, and recognizing the need for a more inclusive, equitable and balanced approach to economic growth that promotes sustainable development, poverty eradication, happiness and well-being of all peoples,

1. *Invites* Member States to pursue the elaboration of additional measures that better capture the importance of the pursuit of happiness and well-being in development with a view to guiding their public policies;

2. *Invites* those Member States that have taken initiatives to develop new indicators and other initiatives to share information thereon with the Secretary-General as a contribution to the United Nations development agenda, including the Millennium Development Goals;

3. *Welcomes* the offer of Bhutan to convene a panel discussion on the theme of happiness and well-being during its sixty-sixth session;

4. *Invites* the Secretary-General to seek the views of Member States and relevant regional and international organizations on the pursuit of happiness and well-being and to communicate such views to the General Assembly at its sixty-seventh session for further consideration.

Bibliography

Almeida, Kanya. 2010a. "The G20 in Seoul – Summit or Abyss?" Inter-Press Service, 4 November. [http://ipsnews.net/news.asp?idnews=53461]

―――. 2010b. "New World Development Report Repackages Old Ideas." Inter-Press Service, 11 April. [http://ipsnews.net/news.asp?idnews=55214]

Ban Ki-moon. 2010. "Need for the UN is greater than ever." *The Sydney Morning Herald*, 31 December. [http://www.smh.com.au/opinion/politics/need-for-the-un-is-greater-than-ever-20101230-19b0g.html]

Better Aid. 2010. "Making development cooperation just: Governance principles and pillars." [http://betteraid.org/en/betteraid-policy/betteraid-publications/policy-papers/401-making-development-cooperation-just-governance-principles-and-pillars.html]

Bissio, Beatriz. 2010. "Emerging Powers Cooking Up New International Order." Inter-Press Service, 18 April, Rio de Janeiro. [http://ipsnews.net/news.asp?idnews=51075]

Bretton Woods Project. 2010. "IMF boardroom crisis: Europeans stubbornly cling to chairs." Update, 30 September. [http://www.brettonwoodsproject.org/art-566647]

Caliari, Aldo. 2011. "Multiple multilateralisms in the post-crisis response: UN vs. G20." [http://www.coc.org/files/ACUNSNewsl.pdf]

————. 2010. "Human rights: The post-2015 agenda?" *The Broker*, 22 September. [http://www.thebrokeronline.eu/Blogs/Goal-Posts-What-next-for-the-MDGs/Human-rights-The-post-2015-agenda]

Campaign for Education. 2010. "G-20: Take Action on Financial Transaction Taxes: International Civil Society Statement to the G-20 Leaders Summit in Seoul."

Carin, Barry and Ramesh Thakur. 2008. "Global Governance for a Global Age: The Role of Leaders in Breaking global Deadlocks." *Policy Brief*, Centre for Global Studies and Centre for International Governance Innovation. [http://www.cigionline.org/publications/2008/11/global-governance-global-age-role-leaders-breaking-global-deadlocks]

Chang, Gordon G. 2010. "The End of Multilateralism: Not that it ever really got started." *The Weekly Standard*, 18 January, 15(17). [http://www.weeklystandard.com/articles/end-multilateralism]

Chowdhury, Iftekhar Ahmed. 2010. "The global Governance Group ('3G') and Singaporean Leadership: Can Small be Significant?" ISAS Working Paper, 19 May, Singapore. [http://www.boell.org/downloads/ISAS_3GThe_Global_Governance_Group_19052010134423.pdf]

Civil Society Reflection Group on Global Development Perspectives. 2011. Statement by the Civil Society Reflection Group on Global Development Perspectives on Rio+20 and beyond. Submission to the Rio+20 compilation document. [http://www.uncsd2012.org/rio20/content/documents/Statement%20by%20the%20Civil%20Society%20Reflection%20Group%2031-10-2011.pdf]

Crossette, Barbara. 2010. "The Elephant in the Room. " *Foreign Policy*, January / February. [http://www.foreignpolicy.com/articles/2010/01/04/the_elephant_in_the_room]

Derviş, Kemal. 2005. "Globalization: Key Challenges for Governance and Multilateralism." Keynote speech at The Challenge of Globalization: Reinventing Good Global Governance, 4 November.

————. 2006. "The Rise of Southern Multinationals: Towards a More Inclusive Globalization." UNDP, 20 October.

Desai, Nitin. 2010. "When Two's Company." *The Times of India*, 4 January. [http://articles.timesofindia.indiatimes.com/2010-01-04/ edit-page/28144295_1_china-india-players-chinese-diplomats]

Deutscher, Eckhard. 2010. "The Future of Development Cooperation Hangs in the Balance." InDepth NewsViewpoint, 14 December.

Dykstra, Page. 2011. "EITI 2011: Learning from Success and Challenges." Revenue Watch Institute, New York.

Evans, Alex. 2010. "10 key issues for international development." Presentation to UK International Development Select Committee, 12 October. [http://www.globaldashboard.org/2010/10/12/10-key-issues-for-international-development]

Folbre, Nancy. 2010. "The World's Best Countries for Women." *The New York Times*, 8 March. [http://economix.blogs.nytimes.com/2010/03/08/the-worlds-best-countries-for-women/]

Forman, Johanna Mendelson. 2009. "Investing in a New Multilateralism: A Smart Power Approach to the United Nations." Center for Strategic and International Studies, Washington, DC. [http://csis.org/files/media/csis/pubs/090128_mendelsonforman_un_smartpower_web.pdf]

The Four Nations Initiative on Governance and Management of the UN. 2007. "Towards a Compact: Proposals for Improved Governance and Management of the United Nations Secretariat." Appendices to the report of final proposals by the Four Nations Initiative. [http://www.centerforunreform.org/node/275]

Friedrich Ebert Stiftung. 2009. *The Geneva Scenarios on Global Economic Governance 2020*. Geneva. [http://library.fes.de/pdf-files/bueros/genf/06597-20091026.pdf]

Fukuda-Parr, Sakiko, Terra Lawson-Remer and Susan Randolph. 2009. "An Index of Economic and Social Rights Fulfillment: Concept and Methodology." *Journal of Human Rights, Vol. 8, Issue 3*, pp.195-221.

G-20. 2010. "The G-20 Toronto Summit Declaration." 26-27 June. [http://canadainternational.gc.ca/g20/summit-sommet/2010/toronto-declaration-toronto.aspx?lang=eng&view=d]

Galtung, John. "WeeklyLeaks." 2010. Inter-Press Service, Schwerte, Germany. [http://www.other-news.info/2010/12/weeklyleaks]

Gelb, Leslie. 2009. "We Just Saw the Future." *The Daily Beast*, 20 December. [http://www.thedailybeast.com/articles/2009/12/20/the-new-global-hierarchy.html]

Gowan, Richard. 2010. "The Obama administration and multilateralism: Europe relegated." FRIDE, CEPS and the Heinrich Böll Foundation. [http://www.fride.org/publication/738/the-obama-administration-and-multilateralism-europe-relegated]

Griesgraber, Jo Marie. 2010. "IMF Make Room for Younger Powers." Blog.reuters.com, 16 December. [http://www.new-rules.org/news/in-the-news/313-reuters-blog-imf-make-room-for-younger-powers]

Haass, Richard N. 2010. "The Case for Messy Multilateralism." *Financial Times*, 5 January. [http://www.cfr.org/un/case-messy-multilateralism/p21132]

————. 2009. "The New 'Informal' Multilateral Era." Council on Foreign Relations, interview by Bernard Gwertzman. [http://www.cfr.org/international-organizations/new-informal-multilateral-era/p20275]

Holmen, Hans and Magnus Jirstrom. 2009. "Look Who's Talking! Second Thoughts about NGOs as Representing Civil Society." *Journal of Asian and African Studies, 44(429)*.

Ibbitson, John, and Tara Perkins. 2010. "How Canada made the G20 happen." *The Globe and Mail*, 18 June. [http://www.theglobeandmail.com/news/world/g8-g20/news/how-canada-made-the-g20-happen/article1609690]

International Monetary Fund. 2010. "IMF Launches Trust Fund to Help Countries Improve Tax Policy and Administration." Press Release 10/500, 17 December. [http://www.imf.org/external/np/sec/pr/2010/pr10500.htm]

International Monetary Fund and International Labour Organization. 2010. "The Challenges of Growth, Employment and Social Cohesion." Presented at a joint ILO-IMF conference in cooperation with the office of the Prime Minister of Norway.

International Network for Economic, Social and Cultural Rights. 2010. "Kuala Lumpur Guidelines for a Human Rights Approach to Economic Policy in Agriculture." New York. [http://www.escr-net.org/actions_more/actions_more_show.htm?doc_id=1431754]

Inter-Press Service. 2010. "South Africa Makes Its Debut at BRICS Summit." 12 April. [http://www.ibsanews.com/south-africa-makes-its-debut-at-brics-summit]

Ishizawa, Jorge. 2011. "Buen Vivir (Good Living) and the Cultural Question." September, PRATEC.

Khor, Martin. "Strange outcome of Cancun climate conference." *The Star*, Malaysia, 13 December. [http://thestar.com.my/news/story.asp?file=/2010/12/13/focus/7611715&sec=focus]

Kollewe, Julia. 2010. "Global unemployment to trigger further social unrest, UN agency forecasts." Guardian.co.uk, 1 October. [http://www.guardian.co.uk/business/2010/oct/01/job-market-recession-social-unrest-ilo]

La Via Campesina, FIAN, Land Research Action Network and Grain. April 2010. "Stop Land Grabbing Now!" [http://www.grain.org/bulletin_board/entries/4224-stop-land-grabbing-now]

Lawson, Max. 2010. "How fertiliser subsidies have transformed Malawi." Oxfam Great Britain, Decmber. [http://www.oxfamblogs.org/fp2p/?p=4187]

Leahy, Stephen. 2010. "North-South Divide Again Clouds Biodiversity Talks." Inter-Press Service, 19 October, Nagoya, Japan. [http://ipsnews.net/news.asp?idnews=53212]

Liddle, Roger. 2010. "Is Social Democracy in Need of a New Economic Model?" 8 December. [http://www.policy-network.net/articles_detail.aspx?ID=3923]

Lynch, Colum. 2010. "U.N. is at a critical juncture as it struggles to assert its relevance." *The Washington Post*, 19 September.

[http://www.washingtonpost.com/wp-dyn/content/article/2010/09/19/AR2010091904764.html]

Malaysian Ministry of Foreign Affairs. Multilateral Diplomacy. [http://www.kln.gov.my/web/guest/md]

Marks, Stephen P., ed. 2008. *Implementing the Right to Development: The Role of International Law.* Friedrich Ebert Stiftung, Geneva. [http://library.fes.de/pdf-files/bueros/genf/05659.pdf]

Martens, Jens. 2010a. *In Search of Buen Vivir.* 11 January. Inter-Press Service. [http://ipsnews.net/news.asp?idnews=54090]

———. 2010b. "Thinking Ahead: Development Models and Indicators of Well-being Beyond the MDGs. International Policy Analysis," Friedrich Ebert Stiftung. [http://library.fes.de/pdf-files/iez/global/07661.pdf]

Mattoo, Aaditya and Arvind Subramanian. 2008. "Multilateralism beyond Doha." Working Paper Series, Peterson Institute for International Economics. [http://www.petersoninstitute.org/publications/wp/wp08-8.pdf]

Mayor, Federico, Marti Olivella and Roberto Savio. 2010. "Manifesto 2010: For a Habitable World for All." [http://www.other-news.info/2010/12/18]

Medicins Sans Frontieres. 2010. "Europe! Hands off Our Medicine." [http://www.doctorswithoutborders.org/publications/article.cfm?cat=briefing-documents&id=4790]

Mitchell, Tom and Simon Maxwell. 2010. "Defining climate compatible development." Policy Brief from the Climate and Development Knowledge Network. [http://ccsl.iccip.net/defining_climate_compatible_development.pdf]

Montreal International Forum. 2009. "Democratizing Global Governance: Principles for the Engagement of Civil Society Organizations with Multilateralism." 3 November, Montreal. [http://www.fimcivilsociety.org/en/library/CS%20Principles%20for%20Good%20Practice_FIM_FINAL.pdf]

Natsios, Andrew. 2010. "The Clash of the Counter-bureaucracy and Development." Center for Global Development. November. [http://www.cgdev.org/files/1424271_file_Natsios_Counterbureaucracy.pdf]

New Rules for Global Finance. 2010. "Open Letter to IMF Governors." 28 September. [http://www.new-rules.org/news/program-updates/296-open-letter-to-imf-governors]

The New York Times. 2010. "Who's In?" 3 October. [http://www.nytimes.com/2010/10/04/opinion/04mon2.html]

Norris, John. 2010. "The Ambassadors-as-CEOs Model." *Foreign Policy*, 17 December. [http://www.foreignpolicy.com/articles/2010/12/17/the_ambassadors_as_ceos_model]

North, James. 2010. "Haiti's Structural Crisis." *The Nation*, 17 December. [http://www.thenation.com/article/157201/haitis-structural-crisis]

Nye, Joseph S. 2010. "The Pros and Cons of Citizen Diplomacy." *The New York Times*, 4 October. [http://www.nytimes.com/2010/10/05/opinion/05iht-ednye.html?adxnnl=1&adxnnlx=1326208066-KvMMKBhB6rKr2A2N1OvAew]

O'Rourke, Kevin. 2009. "Economic and political multilateralism is more vital than ever." Ft.com/economistsforum, 26 March.

[http://blogs.ft.com/economistsforum/2009/03/economic-and-political-multilateralism-is-more-vital-than-ever/#axzz1j4IUMC78]

Obama, Barack. 2010. "Remarks of President Barack Obama as Prepared for Delivery at the Millennium Development Goals Summit." 22 September, New York. [http://www.usaid.gov/press/speeches/2010/sp100922.html]

Palley, Thomas I. 2010. "Deaf to History's Rhyme: Why President Obama is Failing." Financial Times Economists' Forum, 2 December. [http://blogs.ft.com/economistsforum/2010/12/deaf-to-historys-rhyme-why-president-obama-is-failing/#axzz1j4IUMC78]

Panitchpakdi, Supachai. 2010. "Imbalances and Fragility of the World Economy." September, Inter-Press Service, Geneva. [http://ipsnews.net/newsTVE.asp?idnews=52984]

Penttilä, Risto. "Multilateralism light: The Rise of informal international governance." 2009. Centre for Euroepan Reform EU2020 Essay. London. [http://www.mendeley.com/research/multilateralism-light-rise-informal-international-governance/#page-1]

Phiri, Peter. 2008. "Who Monitors the Monitors?" CIVICUS Legitimacy, Transparency and Accountability Programme. [http://www.civicus.org/content/e-CIVICUS408-Who-monitors-monitors-PeterPhiri.html]

PovertyMattersBlog. 2010. "Why is the Gates Foundation investing in GM giant Monsanto?" 29 September. [http://www.guardian.co.uk/global-development/poverty-matters/2010/sep/29/gates-foundation-gm-monsanto]

Pred, David and Natalie Bugalski. 2011. "Cambodia and the limits of World Bank accountability." Bretton Woods Project, 5 April. [http://www.brettonwoodsproject.org/art-567913]

Principles for Responsible Investment. 2010. "Universal Ownership: Why environmental externalities matter to institutional investors." PRI Association and UNEP Finance Initiative. [http://www.unpri.org/files/uop_long_report.pdf]

Quigley, Bill. 2011. "Robin Hood in Reverse in US–Seven Examples." ZSpace Page. [http://www.zcommunications.org/robin-hood-in-reverse-in-u-s-seven-examples-by-bill-quigley]

Raja, Kanaga. 2010. "Speculation Played Major Role in Food Price Crisis." Third World Network Features. [http://www.twnside.org.sg/title2/susagri/2010/susagri131.htm]

Revenue Watch Institute and Transparency International. 2010. "Revenue Watch Index: First Ranking of Government Openness in Oil, Gas and Mining Management." Press release, 6 October, Washington, DC. [http://transparency.org/news_room/latest_news/press_releases/2010/2010_10_06_revenue_watch_index_2010]

Rieff, David. 2010. "Losing Hearts and Minds: Development and Its Discontents." *The New Republic*, 16 August. [http://www.tnr.com/blog/foreign-policy/77050/losing-hearts-and-minds-development-and-its-discontents]

Rousseff, Dilma. 2010. "Brazil: Continuity and Acceleration." Inter-Press Service/TerraViva, 1 October. [http://www.other-news.info/2010/10/brazil-continuity-and-acceleration]

Roy, Rathin. "South-South Cooperation Must Be Rooted in Policy Dialogue." Inter-Press Service, Brasilia.

Savio, Roberto. 2011. "Europe: The Fiscal Deficit vs. the Social Deficit." Rome. 18 April, Other News. http://www.other-news.info/2011/04/europe-the-fiscal-deficit-vs-the-social-deficit/

————. 2010a. "The Fall of the West." Rome. 17 November, Other News. [http://www.other-news.info/2010/11/the-fall-of-the-west]

————. 2010b. "Reflections on the Current Crisis." Rome. 9 December, Other News. [http://www.other-news.info/2010/12/reflections-on-the-current-crisis]

Schmiegelow Partners. "Which new world order: unipolar? bipolar? multiploar? non-polar?" [http://policyanalysis.wordpress.com/2009/11/23/which-new-world-order-unipolar-bipolar-multipolar-non-polar]

Shen Wei. 2008. "In the Mood for Multilateralism? China's Evolving Global View." Centre Asie Ifri. [http://www.ifri.org/?page=contribution-detail&id=5089&id_provenance=97]

Social Watch. 2010. "Forum on Minority Issues Discusses Participation in Economic Life." [http://www.socialwatch.org/node/12589]

Stiglitz, Joseph E., Amartya Sen and Jean-Paul Fitoussi.2009. "Report by the Commission on the Measurement of Economic Performance and Social Progress." [http://www.stiglitz-sen-fitoussi.fr/documents/rapport_anglais.pdf]

Stratton, Allegra. 2010. "Happiness index to gauge Britain's national mood." *The Guardian*, 14 November. [http://www.guardian.co.uk/lifeandstyle/2010/nov/14/happiness-index-britain-national-mood]

Strauss-Kahn, Dominique. 2009. "Multilateralism and the Role of the International Monetary Fund in the Global Financial Crisis." Speech as the School of Advanced International Studies, Washington, DC, 23 April. [http://www.imf.org/external/np/speeches/2009/042309. htm]

Sumner, Andy. 2010. "The World's Poor Aren't Where We Think They Are." Institute of Development Studies.

UNDP Civil Society Consultation. 2009. Platform HD2010: Towards a People's Multilateralism. 4-5 June, New York. [http://hdr.undp.org/en/media/Civil_society_HDR_2010_4-5-June_2009.pdf]

United Nations Development Programme. 2009. "Equity, sustainability and Peace: Human Development in a Rapidly Changing World." A UNDP Discussion Paper.

United Nations Division for Economic and Social Affairs. 2010a. *Development Cooperation for the MDGs: Maximizing Results.* [http://www.un.org/en/ecosoc/julyhls/pdf10/10-45690_(e)(desa) development_cooperation_for_the_mdgs_max_results.pdf]

————. 2010b. "United Nations operational activities for development." UN-DESA Funding Update No. 1. June. [http://www.un.org/esa/coordination/funding_note.pdf]

————. 2010c. *World Economic and Social Survey 2010: Retooling Global Development.* [http://www.un.org/esa/policy/wess/wess2010files/wess2010.pdf]

United Nations Division for Public Administration and Development Management. 2008. "Contribution of Decentralized Cooperation to Decentralization in Africa." ST/ESA/PAD/SER.E/125. [http://www.euroafricanpartnership.org/contributi/DCStudy-publication-7_08.pdf]

United Nations General Assembly. 2010a. "Draft resolution submitted by the President of the General Assembly: System-wide coherence." A/64/L.56, 30 June.

————. 2010b. "Letter dated 11 March 2010 from the Permanent Representative of Singapore to the United Nations addressed to the Secretary-General." A/64/706.

United Nations Research Institute for Social Development. 2010. *Combating Poverty and Inequality: Structural Change, Social Policy and Politics*. [http://www.unrisd.org/publications/cpi]

United Nations Secretary-General. 2010. The Secretary-General's Retreat, Background Papers, Alpbach, 5-6 September. [http://www.scribd.com/doc/37334987/The-Secretary-General-s-Retreat-Sept-2010-background-papers]

United Nations University and Government of Catalonia. 2009. "Decentralized Governments and the New Multilateralism." 19 October. [http://www.ony.unu.edu/events-forums/new/WWNY/2009/regional-organizations-and-mul.php]

Van Zyl, Albert. 2011. "Can We Deep Throat Our Way to Governance Accountability?" Budgets for People Blog, 19 April. [http://openbudgetsblog.org/2011/04/19/can-we-deep-throat-our-way-to-governance-accountability]

Vidal, John. 2011. "Bolivia enshrines natural world's rights with equal status for Mother Earth." *The Guardian*, 11 April, La Paz. [http://www.guardian.co.uk/environment/2011/apr/10/bolivia-enshrines-natural-worlds-rights]

Vos, Rob. 2010. "Retooling Global Development." United Nations Division for Economic and Social Affairs. [www.un.org/esa/policy/wess/wess2010files/wess2010.pdf]

Wade, Robert and Jakob Vestergaard. 2010. "Overhaul the G20 for the sake of the G172." *Financial Times*, 21 October. [http://www.ft.com/intl/cms/s/0/a2ab4716-dd45-11df-9236-00144feabdc0.html#axzz1jLDsoBrz]

Witcher, Tim. 2010. "UN launches $40 billion health drive." AFP, 21 September. [http://www.google.com/hostednews/afp/article/ALeqM5jZGy1n7Fbe2lzQ4TPmbjO3wi32SQ]

Wolf, Martin. 2010. "Basel: the mouse that did not roar." *Financial Times*, 14 September. [http://www.ft.com/intl/cms/s/0/966b5e88-c034-11df-b77d-00144feab49a.html#axzz1jLDsoBrz]

World Economic Forum Ad Hoc Working Group on Trade and Climate Change. 2010. *From Collision to Vision: Climate Change and World Trade.* [http://www3.weforum.org/docs/WEF_ClimateChange_WorldTradeDiscussionPaper_2010.pdf]

Endnotes

1. UN Charter, preamble and article 55 [www.un.org/en/documents/charter].

2. The 20 members of the G-20 include Argentina, Australia, Brazil, Canada, China, France, Germany, India, Indonesia, Italy, Japan, Mexico, Russia, Saudi Arabia, South Africa, Republic of Korea, Turkey, the United Kingdom, the United States of America and the European Union. Additional countries and multilateral institutions are usually invited to participate.

3. June 2010 communiqué [www.g20.org/Documents/g20_declaration_en.pdf].

4. Seoul communiqué [www.g20.org/Documents2010/11/seoulsummit_declaration.pdf].

5. Desai, 2010.

6. Agenda 21 recognizes that broad public participation in decision-making is one of the fundamental prerequisites for the achievement of sustainable development, and identifies specific roles and responsibilities for nine major groups of civil society: women, children and youth, indigenous people, non-governmental organizations, local authorities, workers and trade unions, business and industry, scientific and technological communities, and farmers.

7. See, for example, the Convention on the Elimination of All Forms of Discrimination against Women [www.un.org/womenwatch/daw/cedaw/cedaw.htm], the Declaration on the Rights of Indigenous Peoples [www.un.org/esa/socdev/unpfii/en/declaration.html], and the Convention on the Rights of Persons with Disabilities [http://www.un.org/disabilities/default.asp?id=150].

8. Evans, 2010.

9. International Organization for Migration [www.iom.int/jahia/Jahia/about-migration/facts-and-figures/lang/en]. See also: United Nations Department of Economic and Social Affairs, Trends in International Migrant Stock: The 2008 Revision [http://esa.un.org/migration/index.asp?panel=1].

10. International Telegraph Union, 2011 [http://world2011.itu.int/sites/default/files/pdf/Social%20Media%20for%20Social%20Change.pdf].

11. The Four Nations Initiative on Governance and Management of the UN 2007.

12. Panitchpakdi, 2010, Inter-Press Service.

13. International Monetary Fund and International Labour Organization, 2010 [www. osloconference2010.org/discussionpaper.pdf]. See also UNCTAD's *Trade and Development Report 2010* [www.unctad.org/en/docs/tdr2010_en.pdf] and the Report of the Commission of Experts of the 64th President of the UN General Assembly on Reforms of the Financial and Monetary System, 2009, [www.un.org/ga/president/63/interactive/financialcrisis/PreliminaryReport210509.pdf].

14. The Decent Work Agenda calls for orienting economies around producing jobs and sustainable livelihoods, guaranteeing workers' rights, putting social protection mechanisms in place, and encouraging independent organizations for workers and employers to freely engage in dialogue [www.ilo.org/global/about-the-ilo/decent-work-agenda/lang--en/index.htm].

15. Sumner, 2010.

16. Sumner, A. and Kanbur, R., 2011, *The Guardian*, "Why give aid to middle-income countries?" [http://www.guardian.co.uk/global-development/poverty-matters/2011/feb/23/aid-to-middle-income-countries].

17. United Nations Division for Economic and Social Affairs, 2010a.

18. OECD, 2010, *2010 DAC Report on Multilateral Aid* [http://www.oecd.org/dataoecd/23/17/45828572.pdf].

19. Bretton Woods Project, 2010, "Fueling Contradictions: The World Bank's energy lending and climate change" [http://www.brettonwoodsproject.org/art-566198].

20. The International Labour Organization's annual conferences bring together tripartite national delegations composed of representatives of social/employment ministries, workers and employers associations, producing very different policy frameworks than those produced on the same issues by institutions represented exclusively by finance ministries and Central Banks. See, for example, www.ilo.org/global/about-the-ilo/who-we-are/tripartite-constituents/lang--en/index.htm.

Authors' biographies

Barbara Adams

Barbara Adams is a Senior Fellow with Global Policy Forum - Europe. She was trained as an economist and served as Executive Director of the Manitoba Council for International Affairs from 1977–1979 in Canada. She worked as Associate Director of the Quaker United Nations Office in New York (1981–1988), where she worked with delegates, UN staff and NGOs on issues of economic and social justice, women, peace and human rights. She served as Deputy Coordinator of the UN Non-Governmental Liaison Service (NGLS) through the period of the UN global conferences and until 2003. From 2003–2008 she served as Chief of Strategic Partnerships and Communications for the United Nations Development Fund for Women (UNIFEM).

Her recent experiences have included being a member of the President of the UN General Assembly's Civil Society Task Force for the 2010 MDG Summit, the Civil Society Reflection Group on Global Perspectives and the Coordinating Committee of Social Watch.

During her career she has worked as a consultant to UNICEF, served on the board of directors for the Canadian Council for International Cooperation (CCIC) and has undertaken development work in Latin America, including on housing and settlement projects in Uruguay.

Barbara Adams has authored and co-authored many articles, reports and booklets on the UN, including *Accounting for Africa at the United Nations: A Guide for Non-Governmental Organizations*;

and *Putting Gender on the Agenda: A Guide to Participating in UN World Conferences.* Her latest publication, co-authored with Gretchen Luchsinger, is *Climate Justice for a Changing Planet: A Guide for Policy Makers and NGOs.*

Gretchen Luchsinger

Gretchen Luchsinger was trained as a writer at Columbia University before working as a journalist with Newsweek International. In 1994, she joined the Women's Feature Service in New Delhi, coordinating coverage on gender and development for mainstream media outlets, and managing the production of daily newspapers at the series of UN development conferences in the 1990s.

Since 1999, she has worked as an independent writer and editor covering UN intergovernmental negotiations and development programmes. Based in New York, she has travelled extensively to profile UN country programmes, with an emphasis on post-conflict States. She has produced publications and websites on a spectrum of current political, development and communication issues for different branches of the United Nations, including UN Women, the UN Development Programme, the Human Development Report Office and the UN Children's Fund. In addition to the NGLS publication *Climate Justice for a Changing Planet* produced in late 2009, she has been engaged in issues related to elections, decentralization, violence against women, and gender and economics.

United Nations Non-Governmental Liaison Service (NGLS)

The United Nations Non-Governmental Liaison Service (NGLS), established in 1975, is a jointly financed interagency programme of the UN system. NGLS promotes constructive relations between the United Nations and civil society, including through dynamic partnerships to foster greater coherence around cross-cutting and emerging issues on the UN's agenda and by facilitating meaningful civil society engagement in UN processes.

Drawing on its inter-agency nature and UN system-wide perspective, NGLS provides strategic information, analysis and support to a wide range of constituencies, using its unique convening and networking capacity to strengthen multistakeholder dialogue and alliance-building on core UN issues. NGLS programme activities deal with the full UN agenda on economic and social development, human rights, environment, peace and security and operate across the entire UN system of agencies, programmes, funds and departments concerned with these issues. NGLS works with national and regional NGOs from developing and industrialized countries and international NGOs.

The information produced by NGLS – both in published form and electronically – combines public information on UN and NGO events and issues, practical "how to" guides to the UN system for NGOs, and substantive analysis of issues on the international agenda. All NGLS publications are available on its website (www.un-ngls.org).

In 2011, the work of NGLS was supported by:

- United Nations Department for Economic and Social Affairs (UN/DESA)
- United Nations Conference on Trade and Development (UNCTAD)
- International Labour Office (ILO)
- United Nations Development Programme (UNDP)
- United Nations Environment Programme (UNEP)
- United Nations Population Fund (UNFPA)

NGLS also receives financial support for its activities from the Governments of Catalonia, Finland, Germany, the Netherlands and Switzerland.

For further information:

NGLS Geneva
Palais des Nations
CH-1211 Geneva 10 Switzerland
Telephone: +41-22/917 2076
Fax: +41-22/917 0432
E-mail: ngls@unctad.org

NGLS New York
Room DC1-1106
United Nations, New York NY 10017, USA
Telephone: +1-212/963 3125
Fax: +1-212/963 8712
E-mail: ngls@un.org